The Art of Business

Ancient Strategy For Modern Entrepreneurs

Michael Miller, Ph.D.

Newest Other Titles

PYRAMID PRESS

pyramidpress.net

And What is Hell? — A True Story As Told by Sara Ramsey and Written by Dorothy Ramsey

A Time of War — Michael Peterson

Child Abuse in America
Coach Miller's Wisdom and Guide to Coaching Success
The Adventures of Steamo the Wonder Crab
The Love of Dogs
The Art of Business
The Art of the Chair
The Art of Coaching Basketball
The Art of the Whistle
The Art of Writing — Michael Miller, Ph.D., M.ED., M.S.

Don't Worry, Be Happy, An Amazing Journey of a Life Well Lived — Dr. Luther C. Guynes, Ph.D. with Scott Schultz

Dr. Luther C. Guyne's Wisdom On Life, Business & Management
Peter Drucker's System of Management in a Business Environment
Bits & Pieces of a Lasting Legacy
Dr. Lou's Journey — Dr. Luther C. Guynes, Ph.D.

Shike Last of the Zinja
Shike Time of The Dragons — Robert Shea

Under the Shadow of Death — Garabed Hagop Aaronian (Aharonian)

Children's Books By Michael Miller, Ph.D., M.ED., M.S.
The Courage and Kindness Series

Elijah's Mark | **Jordan's Reach** | **Kenji's Courage** | **Liam's Smile**
Maya's Listening Light | **Sophie's Steps** | **The Kindest Goodbye**

The Art of Business

Ancient Strategy For Modern Entrepreneurs

Michael Miller, Ph.D.

PYRAMID PRESS

LOS ANGELES, CALIFORNIA U.S.A.

ISBN 13: 978-1-971241-03-6
ISBN 10: 1-971241-03-2

Pyramid Press First Edition 2026

The paper used in this publication meets the minimum requirements
of the American National Standard for Permanence of
Paper for Printed Library Materials Z39.48-1984

Printed in USA

PYRAMID PRESS

2046 Hillhurst Avenue
Los Angeles, CA 90027
contact@pyramidpress.net

Dedication

To those who accept responsibility willingly. To the people who understand that building anything worthwhile–a business, a career, an organization, or a meaningful life–requires sacrifice long before it produces reward.

To the small business owners who carried the pressure quietly. Who stayed open when the numbers said otherwise. Who made difficult decisions with incomplete information. Who learned that survival itself is sometimes an achievement.

To the operators, managers, entrepreneurs, and builders who discovered that success is rarely built through inspiration. It is built through repetition. Through pressure. Through discipline maintained long after emotion disappears. And it begins with a truth most people underestimate:

"A beginning is more than half of the whole."

Because the hardest step is rarely mastering the process. It is starting despite uncertainty. Starting before conditions feel perfect. Starting before fear disappears.

This book is dedicated to those who kept going anyway. The people who remained disciplined while others chased hype. Who solved problems instead of announcing them. Who adapted instead of making excuses. Who stayed emotionally steady while others became distracted, discouraged, reactive, or afraid. The people who understood that meaningful achievement requires endurance long before recognition arrives.

Most victories are constructed quietly–through ordinary decisions made correctly and consistently over long periods of time. And the people who ultimately succeed are usually not the most gifted. They are the ones who became difficult to discourage. They endure longer. They focus longer. They sacrifice longer. They stay committed longer.

While others wait for ideal conditions, they continue building. And in time, that persistence separates them from the crowd.

And to Jimmy Britt and Kevin Jackson–two small business owners who continue building their businesses and their brands through uncertainty, pressure, sacrifice, and responsibility. Men who continue showing up, solving problems, making difficult decisions, and carrying burdens most people never see or appreciate. Men who know that meaningful achievement is rarely dramatic while it is being built.

This book is for them–and for all those who continue building anyway.

May it strengthen their resolve, sharpen their judgment, and remind them that endurance is often the greatest competitive advantage of all.

–Michael Miller, Ph.D.

Preface

Business, like competition in sport, is rarely decided by luck. It is decided by preparation, discipline, and the ability to make clear decisions when conditions are uncertain. Many entrepreneurs believe success comes from ideas. In reality, success comes from execution. A great idea without discipline fails. A simple idea executed with clarity and persistence often succeeds.

Throughout history, leaders in many fields have studied the principles of strategy–how to prepare before competition begins, how to understand opponents, how to lead groups of people toward a common goal, and how to adapt when circumstances change.

Those principles apply just as clearly to business as they do to any other competitive environment. Markets shift. Competitors react. Resources are limited. Decisions must often be made with incomplete information. In those conditions, the entrepreneur must become a strategist.

This book applies timeless strategic ideas to the modern challenge of building and sustaining a small business. It is not a book about quick profits or shortcuts. It is about the discipline required to build something that lasts.

A business built on preparation, clear leadership, sound systems, and intelligent adaptation can survive competition, economic cycles, and unexpected challenges.

The goal of this book is simple: To help entrepreneurs build businesses that endure.

–Michael Miller, Ph.D.

Table of Contents

Introduction

Every business begins with a decision.

The decision to step forward when others hesitate.

The decision to accept responsibility instead of security.

The decision to risk failure in pursuit of independence and achievement.

Entrepreneurship is not simply the act of starting a company. It is the act of entering a competitive arena where preparation, discipline, and judgment determine survival. Markets reward clarity and punish confusion. Competitors respond quickly to weakness. Resources are always limited, and time is never on the side of the unprepared.

For many entrepreneurs, the journey begins with an idea–a product, a service, or a vision of doing something better than it has been done before.

But ideas alone do not build businesses.

Every year countless businesses begin with enthusiasm and promise. Many of them fail not because the founders lacked intelligence or effort, but because they lacked strategy. They entered the marketplace without fully understanding the environment they were stepping into. They underestimated competition, overestimated demand, or exhausted their resources before the business had time to grow.

Business, in many ways, is a competitive arena. Companies compete for customers, resources, attention, and market position. Decisions must often be made quickly and with incomplete information. Conditions change unexpectedly. Competitors react. Markets evolve.

In such an environment, success rarely belongs to those who move first or speak the loudest. Instead, it belongs to those who prepare carefully, observe clearly, and act with disciplined intention.

Throughout history, leaders have studied the principles of strategy to understand how success is achieved in competitive environments. These principles focus on preparation, understanding one's environment, managing resources wisely, and recognizing opportunities before others do.

While these ideas were often discussed in military or political contexts, they apply equally well to business. Entrepreneurs face similar challenges: limited resources, strong competition, unpredictable conditions, and the need to make decisions that will shape long-term outcomes.

The purpose of this book is to explore how those strategic ideas apply to the modern entrepreneur.

The goal is not to present complicated theories or abstract models. Instead, the focus is on practical strategic thinking–how to prepare before entering a market, how to structure a business for stability, how to allocate resources wisely, and how to adapt when conditions change.

Small businesses, in particular, benefit from strategic clarity. Large corporations often survive mistakes because they possess deep resources and established market positions. Small businesses rarely have that luxury. A few poor decisions, poorly timed investments, or misjudged opportunities can place the entire enterprise at risk.

For that reason, the small business owner must think strategically from the very beginning.

A sustainable business is not built on speed or excitement. It is built on preparation, patience, and intelligent decision-making. Entrepreneurs who understand their market, manage resources carefully, and establish clear systems create businesses that can endure competition and economic cycles.

Another common misconception about business is the belief that growth alone defines success. Many entrepreneurs chase rapid expansion without establishing the systems or leadership structure required to sustain it. In doing so, they create organizations that grow quickly but collapse just as quickly when pressure increases.

The strongest businesses are not necessarily the fastest growing ones. They are the ones built on solid foundations–clear leadership, disciplined operations, strong customer relationships, and a reputation for reliability.

This book is written for entrepreneurs who wish to build businesses that endure.

It is intended for founders starting their first venture, for small business owners seeking greater stability, and for leaders who want to strengthen the strategic foundations of their organizations.

Each chapter examines a different aspect of strategic thinking in business–from understanding the market environment to managing resources, adapting to change, and positioning a company for long-term success.

These ideas are not shortcuts. They are principles that reward patience and discipline.

Entrepreneurship will always involve risk. Markets will fluctuate, competitors will appear, and unexpected challenges will arise. But entrepreneurs who approach business strategically place themselves in a far stronger position to survive those challenges and build something lasting.

In the end, the purpose of a business is not simply to generate profit.

A well-run business creates value for customers, provides stability for employees, strengthens communities, and allows entrepreneurs to turn their vision into reality.

Those who build with discipline and clarity often discover that the true reward of entrepreneurship is not only financial success, but the satisfaction of creating something meaningful and durable.

The chapters that follow explore the strategic principles that make such businesses possible.

ENTER
AT YOUR
OWN RISK

Chapter
1

The Ground of Business:
Before You Enter the Market

Businesses fail in the marketplace
long before they fail on the balance sheet.
–Dr. Michael Miller

I. Verses on the Ground

1. Before an army marches,
   it studies the ground.
2. Before a business opens its doors,
   it must know where it stands.
3. The wise owner chooses ground
   that matches his strength
   and avoids ground
   that magnifies his weakness.
4. Some markets are fertile,
   some are flooded,
   some are poisoned.

Few entrepreneurs look closely enough to know which is which.

5. To enter business without understanding the ground is to fight a war in the dark.
6. The small business cannot afford many mistakes, so its first task is to see clearly.
7. When purpose is clear,
   customers are understood,
   numbers are honest,
   and risk is measured–
   the ground becomes an ally.
8. When purpose is vague,
   customers are imagined,
   numbers are fantasy,
   and risk is ignored–
   the ground itself becomes the enemy.

II. Owner's Commentary

Why "Ground" Matters More for Small Business

In war, "ground" means the physical terrain: hills, rivers, roads, choke points.

In business, ground means:

- The market you're entering
- The customers you intend to serve
- The problem you're solving
- The constraints you face (money, time, skills, location)
- The rules of the game in that industry

Big companies can afford bad ground–they can burn cash, pivot, and survive.

A small business usually gets one or two real shots. You can't waste yours.

This chapter is about everything that must be understood before you sign a lease, hire staff, or print a single business card.

III. Step One: Define Your True Objective

Most people start a business with fuzzy goals:

- "I want freedom."
- "I don't want a boss."
- "I want to make a lot of money."

Those are feelings, not objectives.

For a small, sustainable business, your objective must be specific and measurable. Examples:

- "I want to build a business that pays me $150,000/ year and employs 3 - 5 people, with hours that let me have dinner with my family most nights."
- "I want a business that I can run remotely with one assistant, targeting 20 high-value clients per year."
- "I want a local service business that dominates a 3 - 5 mile radius and can eventually be sold for 3 - 5 × annual profit."

If you don't define your objective, the business will define it for you–often as:

"You work all the time and still don't make enough money."

Action for you:

Write down, in one sentence, what "success" looks like for this business in 3 - 5 years. Not a fantasy–something you can reasonably build.

IV. Choosing Your Battlefield: Niche and Positioning

In *The Art of War*, the general doesn't just say, "We'll fight somewhere over there."

He chooses the exact hill, road, and timing that favor his forces.

For a small business, that means:

1. A specific type of customer
2. A specific problem you solve
3. A distinct way you solve it that others are not doing

1. Who exactly are you serving?

"Everybody" is not a market.

- Not "homeowners." → "Homeowners in older neighborhoods who need major renovations but are afraid of being ripped off."

- Not "people who need tax help." → "Self-employed professionals earning $80 - 300k who hate dealing with IRS paperwork."
- Not "basketball parents." → "Parents of serious high school players who want college exposure and real development, not just tournaments."

The more clearly you see your customer, the easier everything becomes:

- Marketing
- Pricing
- Service design
- Hiring
- Systems

2. What painful problem do you solve?

People don't buy "nice ideas." They buy relief:

- Relief from confusion
- Relief from fear
- Relief from risk
- Relief from hassle
- Relief from embarrassment

Ask:

- What keeps my ideal customer up at night?
- Where do they feel cheated, lost, overwhelmed, or ignored?
- Where are they saying, "I would gladly pay someone to take this off my plate"?

If the problem isn't painful, the business will be.

3. Why you, and not the dozens of others?

This is positioning–how you occupy a unique corner of the market.

Examples:

- “The only remodeling contractor in this area who gives itemized, transparent bids and weekly progress reports.”
- “The youth basketball program that focuses on player IQ and film work, not just tournaments and hype.”
- “The local café that serves high-quality food fast to workers on 30-minute breaks, with an ordering system built around speed.”

You do not need to be better at everything.

You need to be clearly better at something that matters to your specific customer.

V. Understanding the Terrain: Market Reality vs Fantasy

Many small businesses die because their owner fell in love with the idea, not the reality.

Reality questions:

1. How many potential customers actually exist in your radius or niche?

2. How often will they buy? (once, monthly, annually?)
3. What do they currently spend to solve this problem?
4. What are they doing now instead of hiring you?
5. Who are your real competitors? (Sometimes it's not who you think.)

If the numbers don't work on paper, they won't magically work in life.

The smaller the business, the less room there is for wishful thinking.

VI. Your Resources: Army Size, Weapons, and Supply Lines

In war, a general must know:

- How many soldiers he has
- What weapons they carry
- How much food and ammunition can be supplied

In business, your "army" is:

- You (skills, energy, experience)
- Money (savings, credit, partners)
- Time (hours per week you can really put in)
- Relationships (customers, mentors, referral partners)
- Reputation (what people already believe about you)

A common mistake: acting like you have a 500-soldier army when you really have five.

Examples of mismatched ground:

- Signing a huge lease when your cash flow is still theoretical
- Offering every service under the sun when you have one employee
- Competing on price with a national chain when you have two people and a van

Sustainable small business is about choosing a model that your current resources can actually support.

VII. Risk: What Can Kill You?

In *The Art of War*, generals obsess over what could destroy them: ambush, starvation, disease, or terrain they don't understand.

In small business, killers include:

- Fixed costs that are too high (rent, payroll, debt payments)
- Customer concentration (relying on one big client for 60 - 80% of revenue)
- No cash buffer (one bad month and you're underwater)
- Legal or regulatory blind spots (permits, licenses, taxes)

- Owner burnout (the owner becomes the bottleneck and then collapses)

You can't remove risk, but you can design around it:

- Start smaller than your ego wants
- Keep fixed costs low at first
- Aim for many medium clients instead of one monster client
- Build simple systems so the business is not entirely in your head

A small business does not die from one punch.
It dies from a structure that cannot absorb any punches.

VIII. Principles for Choosing Strong Ground

Put this checklist in front of you when evaluating any business idea:

1. Clear, specific customer–You can describe them in one sentence.
2. Painful, real problem–You can hear them complaining about it in the wild.
3. Simple, repeatable solution–You're not reinventing the wheel every time.
4. Honest numbers–Revenue, costs, and profit look realistic, not magical.
5. Match with your strengths–Uses what you're actually good at.

6. Low early fixed costs–Business can survive bad months.
7. Path to sustainability–Not a one-time hustle, but an income that can last.

If you can't check most of those boxes, the ground is shaky.

IX. Exercises for This Chapter

1. Write Your Objective

One sentence:

"In 3 - 5 years, I want this business to ______________________________."

2. Define Your Ideal Customer

- Age, income, location, mindset
- What they care about
- What they fear

3. Name the Pain

Write three sentences finishing:

- "They're sick of…"
- "They wish someone would just…"
- "They would happily pay to avoid…"

4. List Your Real Resources

- Cash available to invest (not fantasy)
- Weekly hours you can truly commit
- Skills and experience you already have
- People who might support or refer you

5. Name Three Big Risks

For your idea, what could actually kill the business? For each, write one thing you can do to reduce that risk.

X. Closing Verses

The small business owner
who studies the ground
saves himself from many invisible enemies.

He chooses markets he can survive in,
customers he can truly serve,
risks he can endure.

When the ground is well chosen,
even a small army can win.

When the ground is chosen in haste,
even a great idea falls into ruin.

Chapter
2

The Cost of Entry: Waging Business Wisely

A wise entrepreneur counts the true cost
of every move before entering the market.
–Dr. Michael Miller

I. The Burden of Business

Before a business earns its first dollar, it must spend many.

Success requires understanding:

- What must be spent
- When it must be spent
- Why it must be spent
- And how fast money can drain when mismanaged

Many entrepreneurs fail not because they have a bad idea–but because they misjudge the true cost of entering the market.

Business is not defeated by competitors first.
It is defeated by cash flow.

II. The Principle of Sustainable Start-Up

Sun Tzu teaches that prolonged warfare exhausts an army.

In business:

- Prolonged start-up phases exhaust savings
- Excessive debt suffocates growth
- Unnecessary expenses drain momentum
- Overbuilding before revenue is fatal

The wise entrepreneur keeps overhead low,
expansion measured,
and operations simple.

A business should grow like a tree:
Steady, rooted, reaching upward with strength–
not like a firework that burns bright and dies quickly.

III. Investing Like a Commander

A good general does not waste resources.
A good business owner does not waste capital.

Spend on what produces revenue:

- Product
- Marketing
- Customer experience
- Systems that reduce labor and increase output
- Compliance that prevents fines and disasters

Spend last on:

- Fancy offices
- Emotional purchases
- Status symbols
- Things meant to impress rather than produce

Every dollar must serve a strategic purpose.

IV. The Cost of Speed vs. The Cost of Delay

In both war and business:

- Acting too slowly allows rivals to gain ground
- Acting too quickly causes costly mistakes

Speed must be balanced with preparation.

Move swiftly when:

- Competitors are asleep
- The opportunity window is small
- Demand is rising
- You have verified your assumptions

Move cautiously when:

- You lack information
- The market is unclear
- The financial cost of failure is high

The entrepreneur must master timing, not just action.

V. Efficiency as a Strategic Weapon

Sun Tzu advises minimizing waste.

In business, waste appears as:

- Time lost in poor processes
- Money lost in poor planning
- Labor lost in unclear instructions
- Reputation lost in poor execution

A small business can outperform giants
if it eliminates inefficiency faster than they do.

Efficiency multiplies strength.

VI. The Psychology of Cost

The greatest mistake entrepreneurs make is emotional spending.

They believe:

- “More money will fix the problem.”
- “Growth means spending more.”
- “If I expand, customers will come.”

But business is not a casino–
and spending does not create success.
Strategy does.
Mastering the emotional side of spending
is as important as mastering the financial side.

VII. The Law of Financial Survival

Your business must be built to survive its hardest months.

A wise entrepreneur keeps enough reserves to withstand:

- Slow seasons
- Market shifts
- Delayed payments
- Unexpected expenses
- Temporary downturns

A business that survives long enough
almost always finds a way to win.

Endurance is a superpower.

VIII. Final Counsel of Chapter 2

The cost of business is not simply money.
It is focus, discipline, clarity, and long-term vision.

A leader who understands the true cost of entry
does not fear the journey–
he respects it.

Master this chapter, and you will never again be blindsided by the financial realities of success.

INTEGRITY
judgment
COMPETENCE
VISION
PERSISTENCE
HUMILITY

Chapter

3

The Moral Code of Leadership

Employees follow clarity and character
long before they follow authority.
–Dr. Michael Miller

Code of Leadership

A leader's strength is not declared–
it is revealed under pressure.

1. Before a business seeks profit, it must first seek purpose.
   Profit sustains the body; purpose sustains the soul.

2. A leader who does not know what he stands for will fall before the first pressure.

3. Employees follow a paycheck; a team follows a mission.

4. The business that lacks a moral code will suffer decay from within before it faces threats from without.

5. The leader must embody consistency, fairness, courage, and restraint.
   For a team mirrors the temperament of its leader.

6. A company where promises are broken
   invites customers to flee.
   A company where promises are honored invites customers to stay.

7. Culture grows from daily action, not slogans.
   Integrity grows from quiet decisions, not speeches.

8. Let the leader's word be trusted.
   Let the leader's standards be unwavering.
   Let the leader's purpose be understood.

9. Where the leader lacks discipline, waste will follow.
   Where the leader lacks vision, confusion will spread.
   Where the leader lacks courage, the business will die from retreat.

10. When the leader is aligned with the mission,
    the team becomes aligned with the leader.
    When the team is aligned, the business becomes unstoppable.

Modern Business Commentary

The Practical Interpretation for Today's Entrepreneur

I. The Moral Foundation of a Small Business

Big companies can survive incompetence, confusion, and weak leadership.

Small businesses cannot.

A small business is fragile. Its leadership either:

- Creates momentum, trust, and clarity

or

- Creates chaos, fear, and inconsistency

Your "moral code" is your leadership philosophy, and it includes:

- How you treat customers
- How you speak to employees
- How you resolve problems
- How you make decisions under pressure
- What you tolerate
- What you refuse to tolerate

This philosophy becomes the identity of the business.

II. The Five Virtues of a Small-Business Leader

1. Consistency

   Employees don't follow unpredictable leaders.

   Consistency builds trust.

   Trust builds culture.

2. Fairness

   Favoritism destroys culture faster than bankruptcy.

   Fair leaders create loyal teams.

3. Discipline

   A leader who cuts corners teaches employees to cut deeper ones.

   Discipline is contagious.

4. Vision

   If the leader doesn't define where the business is going, the team will drift into confusion.

5. Courage

Courage is required to:

- Raise prices
- Fire toxic clients
- Eliminate weak employees
- Change failing systems
- Invest when others hesitate

A small business follows the courage of its owner.

III. Culture: The Hidden Force Behind Success

Culture is not inspirational posters or fake core values.

Culture =
The behaviors you reward +
the behaviors you tolerate.

Examples:

- If you reward punctuality → You get reliability

- If you tolerate laziness → You get excuses
- If you confront problems quickly → You prevent rot
- If you avoid confrontation → The business slowly dies

Culture becomes your competitive advantage in a crowded market.

IV. Leadership as a Service to Your Business

True leadership is not dominance–it is responsibility.

Your business is a living organism that depends on your:

- Focus
- Clarity
- Organization
- Accountability
- Emotional stability

Your business follows your emotional patterns:

- If you are frantic → operations become frantic
- If you are calm → customers feel it
- If you are decisive → your staff moves with confidence
- If you are scattered → everything becomes inefficient

Leadership is not just running the business.

Leadership is being the business.

V. The Business That Earns Trust Earns Survival

When customers trust you:

- They forgive mistakes
- They refer others
- They stay loyal
- They pay premium prices

Trust acts as your business's financial shield.

The fastest way to fail as a small business is to break:

- Promises
- Deadlines
- Quality standards
- Professional boundaries

Trust is the currency of survival.

Summary

In small business, your leadership code replaces the army's "moral law."

It binds people together, clarifies decisions, and defines the business's fate.

A leader with discipline, vision, fairness, courage, and consistency can grow a business from nothing.

A leader without them will destroy a business–even if the idea was brilliant.

Chapter
4

Setting Up Your Business to Win Before Day One

The structure of a business determines its future before the first customer ever arrives.

–Dr. Michael Miller

Tactical Positioning: Building Defense Before You Compete

In the language of strategy: invincibility comes from preparation; opportunity comes from the market.

Before a business seeks growth, it must first secure stability.

Before you pursue customers, you must protect your foundation.

Before you attempt advantage, you must eliminate vulnerability.

Success is engineered. Failure is permitted.

I. The Invisible Foundation

The public sees the brand–the logo, the website, the product.

But the real business–the one that determines survival–is invisible.

This foundation determines:

- How fast you can grow
- How much stress you can endure
- How many mistakes you can absorb
- How much profit you keep

If this foundation is weak, the business collapses under its own weight.

II. The Principle of Defensive Readiness

In business, defense is not passivity–It is preparation.

Every small business carries inherent faultlines–hidden weaknesses that if exposed or exploited, can unravel the entire enterprise.

Common points of failure:

- Too few customers
- Too few revenue streams
- Lack of key employees
- Poor bookkeeping
- Inconsistent cash flow

- Overreliance on one supplier
- Poor recordkeeping or compliance

Your task is precise:

Identify what can break.

Understand why it can break.

And eliminate it before it does.

III. Eliminating Points of Failure

Every business venture has points of vulnerability which if exploited can destroy the project.

Common points of failure:

- Too few customers
- Too few revenue streams
- Lack of key employees
- Poor bookkeeping
- Inconsistent cash flow
- Overreliance on one supplier
- Poor recordkeeping or compliance

Your task is precise:

Identify what can break.

Understand why it can break.

And eliminate it before it does.

IV. Systems as Shields

Systems are the armor of a small business.

A system is:

- Repeatable
- Documented
- Teachable
- Trackable
- Independent of any one person

Before Day One, you should have:

- A defined sales pipeline
- A standardized onboarding workflow
- A clear service delivery process
- A weekly financial review system
- Templates for marketing and communication
- A quality-control checklist

Systems prevent chaos.
Systems allow scale.
Systems defend against uncertainty.
Systems do not just support growth–they protect it.

V. Strengthening the Interior Before Facing the Exterior

Many entrepreneurs rush outward:

- Marketing
- Sales

- Branding
- Expansion

But strategy demands the opposite.
Before external effort, strengthen internally:

- Strengthen cash flow before scaling
- Strengthen operations before advertising
- Strengthen systems before volume
- Strengthen value before pricing

When the inside is solid, the outside becomes easier.

VI. Financial Defense

The most common cause of small business failure is not lack of customers–

it is lack of cash flow.

Before opening, you must have:

- A realistic burn rate calculation
- A 12-month cash flow forecast
- A profit model based on margins, not hope
- A cash buffer for emergencies

Cash is food. Cash is ammunition. Cash is survival.
Revenue is vanity. Cash flow is survival.

VII. Creating Predictability in an Unpredictable Market

The marketplace is volatile. Competitors change. Customers shift.

Your defense is the creation of internal predictability:

- Predictable processes
- Predictable customer experience
- Predictable financial rhythms
- Predictable service quality

VIII. Pre-Launch Momentum

Winning businesses create demand before they open.

Build momentum by:

- Pre-selling services
- Soft-launching to trusted customers
- Building a small audience
- Creating early testimonials
- Forming key partnerships

The launch is not the beginning of the struggle; it is the moment you bring into the light everything you have already built.

Momentum reduces risk before the first transaction.

IX. The First 90 Days Plan

Day One is not the challenge–the first 90 days are.

Before launching, you must have a written plan that includes:

- Daily actions
- Weekly customer acquisition goals
- Revenue targets
- Marketing schedule
- Cost controls
- Review systems

Clarity in the first 90 days prevents confusion for the next 900.

X. The Philosophy of Pre-Launch Excellence

"Victorious entrepreneurs win first and then go to market."

Win in:

- Planning
- Systems
- Financial control
- Discipline
- Clarity

The launch is not the start of the battle; it is the moment you reveal that the victory has already been secured.

Technical Innovation
Inspired Leadership
Sustainable Business
Effective Risk Management
Stakeholder Responsiveness

Chapter 5

The Five Strengths of a Sustainable Business

Purpose, leadership, systems, awareness, and resources are the pillars that hold a business upright.

–Coach Michael Miller

Clarity Before Conflict

Every business rises and falls on two forms of clarity:

1. Itself
2. Its environment

In business, the greatest threat is not competition–it is ignorance.

Ignorance of your market.

Ignorance of your customers.

Ignorance of your competition.

Ignorance of your own strengths and weaknesses.

A business that enters a marketplace without this knowledge may not fail instantly–but the clock is ticking.

I. Know Yourself: The Internal Battlefield

Before studying competitors, you first must master the truth of your own business.

1. What do you actually provide?

Most small businesses fail because the owner cannot articulate what the business really does.

You must clearly define:

- What problem you solve
- Why you solve it better
- Who you solve it for
- How fast you solve it
- Why customers should trust you

If you cannot state this in a single sentence, customers will never figure it out for themselves.

2. Your strengths

Every small business has hidden advantages:

- Speed
- Personal service
- Lower overhead
- Flexibility
- Creativity
- Authenticity

You must know these and weaponize them.

3. Your weaknesses

Small businesses fail when the owner refuses to acknowledge:

- Cash limitations
- Lack of staff
- Lack of systems
- Lack of brand recognition
- Inexperience
- Capacity limits

Weaknesses don't destroy businesses–ignoring them does.

4. Your capacity

The fastest way to collapse is to promise more than you can deliver.

Scale only when your systems allow it.

II. Know Your Customer: The True Center of Battle

Most entrepreneurs imagine their business being built around their dream customer.

But in reality, the market tells you the truth.

1. Who actually needs what you provide?

Not who you wish–who they actually are:

- Age
- Income
- Pain points

- Behavior
- Location
- Buying habits

2. What problem do they desperately need solved?
   People pay for relief from:
   - Stress
   - Fear
   - Confusion
   - Uncertainty
   - Wasted time
   - Wasted money
   - Wasted energy

If you solve a real pain, you will never be without customers.

3. How do they decide to buy?
   Every market behaves differently.

Some buy on:

- Trust
- Speed
- Convenience
- Price
- Expertise
- Brand image

Understand their decision path, and you control the sale.

III. Know Your Competitors: The Terrain You Battle On

Competitors aren't villains–they are maps.

They show you:

- What the market already respects
- What customers hate
- What customers wish existed
- Where the gaps are
- Where you can dominate

1. Study them like a general studies an opposing army

   Know their:

   - Strengths
   - Weaknesses
   - Reviews
   - Pricing
   - Speed
   - Branding
   - Reputation
   - Customer complaints

   The complaints column is your treasure map.

2. Competitors tell you exactly what NOT to do

When you see them:

- Overcharging
- Underperforming

- Ignoring customers
- Being inconsistent
- Posting weak branding
- Delivering slow service
- Treating customers like transactions

…your path becomes obvious.

3. Competitors reveal the untapped gap

There is always a gap in the market:

- Faster
- Cleaner
- More honest
- Better communication
- Better systems
- More flexible
- More trustworthy

The small business that finds the gap becomes the one people talk about.

IV. Know the Market Itself: Seasonal, Emotional, Economic Terrain

The market has terrain just like a battlefield.

1. Seasonal terrain

   Some businesses thrive cyclically.

   Study your slow seasons and fast seasons.

2. Economic terrain

Interest rates, inflation, job markets–this is all battlefield weather.

3. Emotional terrain

Consumer fear changes buying habits.

Consumer excitement creates opportunity.

The greatest businesses read the emotional climate and adapt quickly.

V. Clarity Creates Power

When you know yourself, your customer, your competition, and your market, three things happen:

1. You stop guessing.
2. You stop wasting money.
3. You stop building the wrong thing.

With clarity, small businesses become unstoppable–not because they are the biggest, but because they are the most aware.

Chapter
6

Evaluating Your Business Terrain

A business that understands its terrain
chooses its battles wisely.

–Coach Michael Miller

The Terrain

Every business operates on shifting ground.
The market changes.
The customer changes.
The conditions change.

If you don't understand the ground you are standing on, you will make the wrong move.

Most businesses don't fail because of effort.
They fail because they are fighting on the wrong ground.

A business that misreads its terrain:

- Expands to fast
- Markets to soon
- Lowers prices too quickly

- Hires before it is time
- Refuses to pivot when conditions change

The advantage does not belong to the fastest–
it belongs to the one who understands where he stands.

Below are the *Nine Grounds* of small business, adapted directly from Sun Tzu.

I. Ground One: The "Idea Stage" Ground

This is the stage where the business exists only in your mind.

The danger:

You think planning equals progress.

The truth:

You must choose–very quickly–whether the idea should be executed, paused, or abandoned.

The wise entrepreneur does not get stuck here.

II. Ground Two: The "Early Testing" Ground

You are testing:

- Interest
- Pricing
- Messaging
- Demand
- Competitors
- Customer pain points

This is not the time for perfection.

This is the time for information gathering.

The founder listens more than he speaks.

III. Ground Three: The "Entering the Market" Ground

This is the most dangerous ground for small businesses.

The risks:

- Overspending on marketing
- Underpricing out of fear
- Offering too many services
- Trying to appeal to everyone

On this ground, clarity wins.

You must declare:

- Who you are
- What you offer
- Who you serve
- What problem you solve

Nothing more.

IV. Ground Four: The "Gaining Traction" Ground

Now customers are coming in.
Revenue is inconsistent, but real.

On this ground you must:

- Fix what is broken
- Improve what is clumsy
- Simplify what is confusing
- Strengthen what is working

This is the ground of iteration, not expansion.

The business becomes sturdier here–if you let it.

V. Ground Five: The "Competitors Notice You" Ground

Sun Tzu calls this *"contentious ground."*

Your business now threatens others.

Competitors:

- Copy your messaging
- Lower their prices
- Target your customers
- Mimic your offers

On this ground, panic kills.

The correct strategy:

- Improve your product
- Refine your systems
- Deepen customer relationships

- Do NOT enter a price war

Compete with quality, not noise.

VI. Ground Six: The "Growth Opportunity" Ground

This is the ground of potential expansion.

You may:

- Add new services
- Add a location
- Add staff
- Increase capacity
- Expand marketing
- Shift to higher-quality customers

But Sun Tzu warns:

"Advantage must not be neglected."

Meaning:

Do not expand until your foundation can support expansion.

VII. Ground Seven: The "Overextension" Ground

This is dangerous ground.

Symptoms:

- You work more but earn less
- You have more customers but worse margins
- Systems break

- Customer experience suffers
- You feel overwhelmed

On this ground, the correct action is retreat, not advance.

Simplify.
Cut.
Pause.
Fix.

Regain balance before moving again.

VIII. Ground Eight: The "Stagnation" Ground

Every business eventually hits a plateau.

It is not failure.
It is a signal.
Stagnation tells you:

- Your offer is aging
- Your messaging is outdated
- Your systems need tightening
- Customer needs have changed

This is the ground where reinvention creates longevity.

Do not fear reinvention.
Fear standing still when everyone else is moving.

IX. Ground Nine: The "Dominant Position" Ground

Few small businesses reach this stage.
You:

- Have strong systems
- Generate predictable revenue
- Manage customers efficiently
- Control your market space
- Possess a reputation that carries weight

Now the only threats are:

- Complacency
- Arrogance
- Comfort
- Neglect

Dominance must be defended with humility and discipline.

Conclusion

A small business survives by understanding its terrain.

A small business thrives by choosing the right strategy for the right ground.

The founder who understands where the business stands today knows exactly what to do next.

Strategy becomes obvious.

Action becomes easier.

Success becomes sustainable.

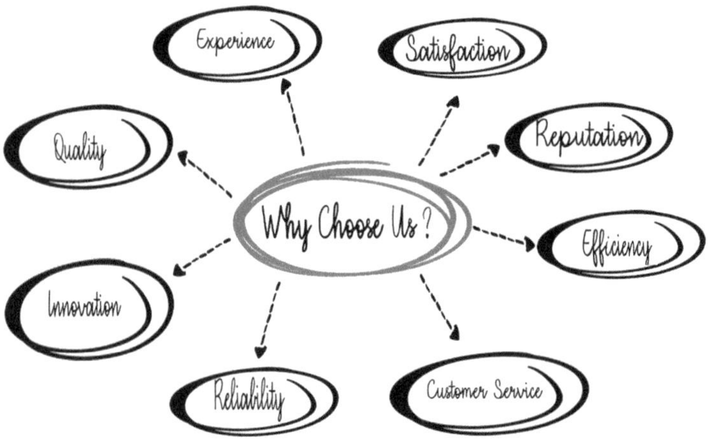
Experience
Satisfaction
Quality
Reputation
Why Choose Us?
Efficiency
Innovation
Reliability
Customer Service

Chapter
7

The Seven Truths That Decide Who Wins in Business

Victory in business belongs to the company that masters the fundamentals others ignore.

–Coach Michael Miller

Before the Outcome is Visible

Before two companies compete, the outcome is often already decided–not by luck, branding, or marketing, but by the seven truths hidden beneath their operation.

These truths determine which business endures and which collapses the moment real pressure arrives.

Every entrepreneur must know them.
Every competitor is measured by them.
These seven truths decide who survives.

I. Who Has the Stronger Purpose?

Sun Tzu: *"Which ruler has the moral law?"*

Customers can feel purpose.

Purpose-driven businesses:

- Communicate clearly
- Serve consistently
- Build loyalty
- Attract better people
- Charge higher prices confidently

Businesses with weak purpose:

- Cheapen themselves
- Chase every customer
- Burn out
- Build nothing lasting

Purpose creates direction.

Purpose creates strength.

Purpose wins.

II. Who Has the Stronger Leadership?

Sun Tzu: *"Which general has the greater ability?"*

Leadership determines culture.

Culture determines performance.

Performance determines survival.

Strong leadership:

- Stays calm during crisis
- Makes clear decisions
- Inspires trust
- Holds standards
- Leads by example

Weak leaders create weak companies.

And weak companies do not last.

III. Who Has the Advantage of Timing?

Sun Tzu: *"Who has Heaven on their side?"*

Timing is one of the most underestimated elements of business.

A good idea at the wrong time loses.

A small idea at the right time wins.

Timing means:

- Market readiness
- Customer mindset
- Economic climate
- Cultural trends
- Technology waves

Victory loves the right moment.

A wise business owner learns to recognize it.

IV. Who Controls Their "Terrain"?

(Sun Tzu: *"Who controls the Earth?"*)

Terrain in business is your environment:

- Costs
- Location
- Tools
- Team strength
- Financial runway
- Customer access

The business that uses its terrain intelligently gains speed and advantage.

The business that ignores its terrain falls behind.

Terrain does not lie.

V. Who Has Better Discipline & Systems?

(Sun Tzu: *"Whose troops have discipline?"*)

Systems beat talent.

Disciplined businesses:

- Deliver consistent quality
- Train employees faster
- Reduce chaos
- Scale smoothly
- Make fewer mistakes

Undisciplined businesses bleed money, time, and trust.

A disciplined small business can defeat a sloppy large one.

VI. Who Has a Clear Advantage Strategy?

(Sun Tzu: *"Whose plan will bring victory?"*)

Every business must answer:

What is our competitive advantage?

Examples:

- Speed
- Quality
- Trust
- Convenience
- Expertise
- Price
- Brand personality
- Story
- Relationships
- Emotional connection

A business without advantage competes on price–and price is the battlefield where small businesses die first.

VII. Who Has the Stronger Will to Win?

(Sun Tzu: *"Which side is more motivated?"*)

In small business, the deciding factor is often endurance.

The business with stronger will:

- Outworks rivals
- Outlasts slow seasons
- Outlearns mistakes
- Outgrows competitors
- Outpersists temporary setbacks

Most businesses die not from failure–
but from the founder giving up too soon.
Willpower is an economic weapon.

Conclusion: The Winner Is Decided Before the Competition Begins

When two businesses enter the same market, these seven truths determine the outcome:

1. Purpose
2. Leadership
3. Timing
4. Terrain
5. Discipline & Systems
6. Advantage Strategy
7. Willpower

The business that aligns these truths gains momentum, clarity, and resilience.

The one that ignores them collapses when pressure arrives.

Victory, in small business as in strategy, begins long before the first customer walks through the door.

Chapter 8

Adapting in Real Time: The Power of Tactical Flexibility

Rigid businesses break; adaptable businesses endure.

–Coach Michael Miller

Speed is Survival

A small business cannot survive–let alone dominate–if it moves slowly.

Markets shift.
Customer behavior changes.
Competitors evolve.
Technology advances.
Unexpected problems appear without warning.

Rigid businesses die.
Flexible businesses thrive.

The small business owner must learn to see reality as it is, not as he wishes it were, and change direction with speed, intelligence, and courage.

This is tactical flexibility.

It is the difference between reacting late…

and staying ahead of everyone else.

I. The Marketplace Will Change– Your Tactics Must Too

Sun Tzu teaches:

"There are roads not to take, and enemies not to fight."

In business, this means:

- Not every trend is worth chasing
- Not every customer is worth saving
- Not every product is worth keeping
- Not every opportunity is actually an opportunity

The danger is stubbornness.

Founders who refuse to change course because:

- They're emotionally attached
- They fear looking wrong
- They don't want to start over
- They don't want to learn something new

…are guaranteed to lose.

Flexibility is not weakness.

It is strategic intelligence.

II. The Three Forms of Tactical Adaptation

Every small business must master three kinds of adaptation:

1. Daily Adaptation: Solving Problems Fast

This includes:

- Fixing customer issues same-day
- Adjusting schedules
- Cleaning up workflow breakdowns
- Redirecting staff
- Switching tools when needed

This is survival-level adaptation.

2. Seasonal Adaptation: Moving With Market Cycles

Every business has seasons:

- Busy periods
- Slow periods
- Times to expand
- Times to pull back
- Times to market hard
- Times to conserve energy

A wise founder tracks patterns and adjusts strategy accordingly.

3. Strategic Adaptation: Reinventing When Necessary

Every 18-36 months a small business must reconsider:

- Pricing structure
- Branding
- Technology
- Products
- Marketing channels
- Hiring needs
- Customer expectations

This is the kind of flexibility that creates longevity.

Businesses that refuse to evolve become relics.

III. When Not to Change Direction

Flexibility does not mean chaos.

The founder must avoid:

- Changing course out of fear
- Switching tactics without data
- Abandoning a strategy too early
- Jumping ship every time something feels difficult

Shallow thinkers pivot constantly.

Disciplined founders pivot only when needed.

A business cannot succeed if it changes strategy every week.

Adaptation must be:

- Precise
- Controlled
- Purposeful
- Based on real-world information

IV. Adapting Without Losing Identity

A business must evolve without losing what makes it unique.

Identity is:

- Your tone
- Your values
- Your promise
- Your commitment to quality
- Your customer philosophy

Tactics change.

Identity stays the same.

The customer must always feel:

"This is who you are. This is what you stand for."

Adapt strategy.

Protect identity.

V. The Courage to Change Quickly

Speed is a weapon.

Most competitors:

- Hesitate
- Overthink
- Delay
- Hope the problem will solve itself
- Get attached to their old way of doing things

Your advantage is simple:

You move faster.

React fast.

Correct mistakes fast.

Change direction fast.
Improve fast.
Learn fast.

Speed creates separation.
The quicker you adjust, the slower your competitors appear.

VI. Detecting the Need to Pivot

Warning signs appear before collapse:

- Declining sales
- Negative customer feedback
- Rising expenses
- Reduced team energy
- Fewer referrals
- Lower engagement
- Conflict between systems and reality

Most founders ignore the signs.

The wise founder investigates early:
"What is this warning telling me?"

Adaptation begins with awareness.

VII. The Strategic Pivot: A Last Resort, Not the First Reaction

A pivot is not a panic move.

A pivot is an intelligent redirection based on:

- Data
- Patterns
- Customer realities
- New opportunities
- Changes in technology
- Shifts in demand

A pivot is:

- Small enough to maintain identity
- Large enough to change destiny

The goal is not to reinvent everything–
Only what needs to evolve.

Conclusion

A sustainable small business is both stable and flexible.

It is rooted in identity, but fluid in tactics.
It stays true to its purpose, but adapts to its environment.
It has strong principles, but light feet.

The business that adapts quickly will always outperform the business that refuses to move.

Just as in The Art of War:

Victory belongs to the business that can change direction faster than its competition.

CASH FLOW
EXPENSES
INCOME

Chapter 9

Managing Cash Flow: Mastering the Lifeblood of Your Business

Cash flow is the oxygen of business–
when it stops, everything stops.

–Coach Michael Miller

Cash is Control

Cash flow is the ground you stand on.
Lose the ground, and your business sinks.
Control the ground, and your business survives anything.

Small businesses do not fail because of lack of ideas.
They fail because the cash stops flowing.

Cash flow is not accounting.
It is survival.

Below are the nine realities–nine "grounds"–of cash flow a small business must learn to read, anticipate, and control.

I. Startup Ground: Cash Out, No Cash In Yet

This is the most dangerous ground for new entrepreneurs.

At the very beginning:

- Money flows OUT
- Customers haven't arrived yet
- Stress is high
- Everything feels uncertain

Most businesses die not because they were bad ideas, but because founders ran out of oxygen before the fire caught.

To survive Startup Ground:

- Lower expenses ruthlessly
- Delay all non-essential spending
- Focus ONLY on actions that directly bring your first revenue

Your first goal is not perfection–
It is momentum.

II. Early Revenue Ground: Money Starts Trickle Flowing In

The trickle gives hope.

But a trickle is not stability.

This phase is where founders make a fatal mistake: They assume early customers = long-term security.

Instead, you must:

- Reinforce what worked
- Track which customers pay fast
- Build repeatable systems around the wins
- Keep expenses low even as revenue grows

Early revenue is "testing ground," not victory ground.

III. Break: Even Ground–The First Real Stability

This is where your business's survival becomes real.

Break-even means:

- All bills paid
- Owner can survive the month
- No panic
- No guessing

But be careful:

Break-even is NOT comfort.
It is the minimum required to avoid collapse.

Smart founders treat break-even as a fragile milestone, not a place to relax.

IV. Momentum Ground: Cash Flow Begins to Build

Momentum ground is powerful.

Revenue is consistent.

Expenses are predictable.

Customers return.

Referrals begin.

This is where many founders sabotage themselves by:

- Expanding too fast
- Hiring too early
- Buying unnecessary equipment
- Raising their personal lifestyle

Momentum is NOT permission to overspend.

Momentum is the moment to strengthen your foundation.

V. Expansion Ground: Opportunities Appear

Sun Tzu wrote:

"Opportunities multiply as they are seized."

Here, cash flow creates new possibilities:

- Hiring
- Adding services

- Opening a second location
- Buying better tools
- Investing in marketing

But expansion is dangerous.

Move too slowly, and competitors catch up.

Move too quickly, and cash drains faster than it comes in.

Expansion requires math, not emotion.

If the numbers don't justify the move, don't move.

VI. Contraction Ground: A Sudden Drop in Cash

Every business faces this.

A slow month…

A lost customer…

A supplier problem…

A seasonal slump…

A personal emergency…

The amateur panics.

The professional tightens, stabilizes, and adjusts.

In contraction:

- Cut expenses fast
- Increase outreach immediately

- Keep existing customers close
- Focus on cash-generating actions ONLY

Contraction is not the end.

It is a test of discipline.

VII. Crisis Ground: Cash Flow Under Attack

This is the battlefield Sun Tzu called *"deadly ground."*

If you do nothing, you die.

If you move with intention, you survive.

Crisis signs:

- Bills due you cannot pay
- Credit running thin
- Customers slowing down
- Stress increasing daily

In crisis:

1. Communicate with creditors
2. Renegotiate payment terms
3. Cut every unnecessary cost
4. Sell unused assets
5. Launch immediate revenue pushes

Crisis ground demands decisive action.

VIII. Recovery Ground: Rebuilding After Damage

Recovery is delicate.

You are still vulnerable, but momentum is returning.

In recovery:

- Restore essential systems
- Rebuild savings
- Strengthen marketing
- Re-evaluate your offerings
- Learn from the crisis

A business that survives a crisis becomes stronger–
If the founder learns, not forgets.

IX. Prosperity Ground: Cash Flow Security

This is the ground small business owners dream of.

Signs of Prosperity Ground:

- Consistent profit
- Predictable income
- Comfortable reserves
- Strong customer loyalty
- Low stress and high confidence

But this ground has its own danger: complacency.

Prosperity is the reward for discipline–

Not the time to abandon it.

Here is where you:

- Reinforce your systems
- Invest in smart growth
- Strengthen your team
- Build long-term resilience
- Prepare for the next down cycle

Prosperity must be protected like a fortress.

Conclusion: Cash Flow Is the True General of Your Business

Master these nine grounds of cash flow, and you can steer your business through any economic climate.

A small business with:

- controlled cash flow,
- steady reserves,
- disciplined spending, and
- consistent incoming revenue

becomes unbreakable.

Cash flow is not numbers.

Cash flow is survival.

Chapter
10

The Element of Deception

The strongest businesses move strategically while their competitors move predictably.

–Coach Michael Miller

Win Before You Are Seen

In business, “deception” does not mean dishonesty.

It means strategic positioning–the ability to hide your moves until they are ready,

to appear small while you build strength,

to confuse competitors while remaining clear to your customers,

to act with speed while others hesitate.

In small business, this is not optional.

It is survival.

I. Move Quietly, Build Loudly

Small businesses lose when they announce too much, too early.

Talking about plans creates:

- Competitors preparing for you
- Customers expecting what you haven't built
- Pressure replacing clarity
- Momentum leaking before you launch

Instead:

Build in silence.
Launch with impact.

Winners prepare in the dark,
and strike in the light.

II. Appear Small While You Grow Strong

Sun Tzu taught that power grows fastest when it is hidden.

For a small business, this means:

- Don't give away your numbers
- Don't overshare your suppliers
- Don't reveal your margins
- Don't brag about your growth targets
- Don't explain your long-term strategy

A small business must protect its early advantages.
Competitors can copy what you show–
but they cannot copy what they never see.

III. Confuse Competitors, Never Customers

Your messaging must be clear to the market and foggy to your competition.

This is the balance:

- Customers receive simplicity
- Competitors receive mixed signals
- The market receives clarity
- Rivals receive confusion

Your customers must know:

- What you offer
- Why it matters
- Why you're different

Your competitors must never fully understand:

- How you deliver
- How you price
- How you scale
- How you train
- How you plan your next move

Clarity to the inside.
Mystery to the outside.

IV. Use Timing to Set Traps

A small business gains leverage when it decides when to act.

Timing traps include:

1. Launching when competitors are asleep
   Holidays, off-seasons, economic dips.

2. Offering specials when rivals raise prices
   You capture trust while they capture anger.

3. Expanding when others contract
   Their fear becomes your advantage.

4. Entering the market right after a competitor fails
   Customers are primed for a replacement.

Timing is invisible strategy.
People see the move,
but never the clock behind it.

V. Never Fight Head-On When You Can Win from the Side

Big businesses prefer straight-line battles:
price wars, advertising wars, space wars.

Small businesses win by:

- Specialization
- Niche domination
- Hyper-specific offerings
- Personalization
- Speed
- Flexibility

Move where the giant is slow.
Attack where the giant is blind.
Serve where the giant cannot care.

Indirect strategy is the small business owner's greatest weapon.

VI. Protect Your Information Like Gold

Your business intelligence includes:

- Costs
- Margins
- Vendor information
- Customer lists
- Trade secrets
- Processes
- Systems
- Marketing data
- Internal policies

Guard it.

A competitor who knows your systems
can build your business
better than you can.

A competitor who knows nothing
cannot copy your path.

VII. Keep Competitors Guessing While Customers Stay Loyal

Deception in business is never aimed at the customer.
It is aimed at the competitor–
the one who wants to take what you build.

Customers get truth.
Competitors get noise.

You earn loyalty with:

- Service
- Integrity
- Consistency
- Personality
- Safety
- Relationship
- Reliability

You confuse competitors with:

- Timing
- Positioning
- Silence
- Speed

- Niche shifts
- Bundles
- Unpredictable moves

A business becomes powerful
when it becomes unreadable.

Conclusion

Deception–in the strategic sense–is not lying.
It is protecting your advantage,
controlling your visibility,
and allowing your business to grow without sabotage.

A small business wins when:

- Competitors misjudge it
- Customers trust it
- The plan stays hidden
- The execution stays sharp
- The timing stays perfect

Appear weak when you are strong.
Appear slow while you gain speed.
Appear small while you build power.

Then, when the moment is right–
strike with unmistakable clarity,
and take the space that others left open.

Chapter
11

The Nine Grounds of Small Business

Every market has its terrain; the wise entrepreneur learns how to fight on each one.

–Coach Michael Miller

Know the Ground. Choose the Move.

Every business operates on different "grounds"– stages, environments, and conditions that demand different tactics.

A small business fails when it uses the wrong strategy for the ground it's standing on.

A founder wins by recognizing the terrain and adapting to it before pressure hits.

Below are the nine modern grounds of small business, and how to win on each.

I. Ground 1: The Idea Ground (Safe Ground)

No real risk.
No customers yet.
No overhead.
No pressure.

Most people stay on Idea Ground forever because it feels comfortable.

Goal on this ground:
Clarify the idea, the market, and the real customer pain–then move.

If you linger too long, momentum dies before it starts.

II. Ground 2: The Testing Ground (Lightly Contested Ground)

This is where you:

- Test pricing
- Test messaging
- Test product fit
- Talk to customers
- Make mistakes cheaply

It's cheap to operate here–but it's also easy to lie to yourself.

Goal:

Find the truth, not confirmation.

III. Ground 3: The Launch Ground (Open Ground)

You have:

- Your first customers
- Your first real expenses
- Your first real problems

Everything feels overwhelming because everything is new.

Goal:

Simplify.

Create one clear offering.

Drive one clear message.

Resist the urge to become "everything to everyone."

IV. Ground 4: The Competitive Ground (Contested Ground)

Customers now compare you to others.

Competitors watch you.

You are no longer invisible.

Here, survival depends on:

- Differentiation
- Customer experience

- Consistency
- Speed

Goal:

Be better at ONE thing than anyone else your customer can find.

That is your wedge.

V. Ground 5: The Reputation Ground (Critical Ground)

This is where your small business becomes known.

Your reputation can start lifting you or drowning you.

Customers begin saying:

- "Try them."
- "Avoid them."
- "They're solid."
- "They're unreliable."

Goal:

Protect your name with your life.

Your brand is the compound interest of every interaction.

VI. Ground 6: The Growth Ground (Difficult Ground)

You are growing–but growth brings chaos.

This ground creates the greatest founder burnout because:

- Systems aren’t built
- Staff isn’t trained
- Lifestyle is disappearing
- Customers are increasing
- Pressure is rising

Goal:

Systemize or die.

The business must stop depending entirely on you.

VII. Ground 7: The Saturation Ground (Encircled Ground)

Your market becomes crowded.

Margins tighten.

Newcomers copy you.

Customers expect more for less.

Most businesses die here because they fail to evolve.

Goal:

Innovate, specialize, or reposition.

Standing still guarantees defeat.

VIII. Ground 8: The Crisis Ground (Desperate Ground)

Every founder faces it:

- Sales drop
- A key employee quits
- A competitor undercuts you
- The economy turns
- You get sick
- Cash runs out

Crisis Ground is where weak businesses disappear–and great businesses transform.

Goal:

Cut fast, simplify, protect cash, and focus on core customers.

Crisis is not the end–it is the reset that forces clarity.

IX. Ground 9: The Freedom Ground (Dominant Ground)

Few small businesses ever reach this stage.

Here you have:

- Systems
- Reputation

- Consistent cash flow
- Loyal customers
- Staff support
- A real foothold in the market

You finally control the business instead of the business controlling you.

Goal:

Guard your discipline.

This is where success makes founders careless.

Freedom Ground is not a finish line–it is a new responsibility.

Conclusion

A small business survives by recognizing the ground beneath it.

A small business grows by adapting to that ground.

A small business thrives by using the right strategy for the right terrain.

When you understand the nine grounds, you stop reacting blindly–and start leading intentionally.

SHORT TERM
MEDIUM TERM
LONG TERM

Chapter
12

Momentum, Expansion, and Long-Term Victory

Momentum belongs to the business that prepares for opportunity before it appears.

–Coach Michael Miller

Build It. Then Let It Carry You.

A small business survives by effort.
A sustainable business grows by strategy.
A dominant business expands by momentum.

Momentum is the invisible force that makes opportunity come easier, customers arrive quicker, and results compound with time.

Momentum cannot be faked.
It must be built, protected, and leveraged deliberately.

This chapter explains how small businesses move from stability → growth → long-term victory.

I. Momentum: The Most Powerful Force in Small Business

Momentum is built when:

- Customers trust you
- Systems run clean
- Word-of-mouth spreads
- Cash flow stabilizes
- The founder makes fewer "fear decisions"
- Wins begin to compound

Momentum is fragile.

The wrong hire, a sloppy month, or a distracted founder can break it instantly.

Momentum thrives on:

- Focus
- Consistency
- Execution
- Customer experience
- Strategic timing

Businesses that continually "stop and restart" never build momentum.

Businesses that stay disciplined eventually become unstoppable.

II. Expansion: Growing Without Destroying What Works

There are two kinds of expansion:

1. Smart Expansion
    - Adding new products that customers already want
    - Expanding only when systems can handle it
    - Growing through proven demand
    - Hiring slowly and deliberately
    - Scaling capacity before marketing

2. Reckless Expansion
    - Expanding too early
    - Chasing new ideas instead of optimizing old ones
    - Hiring employees you can't carry
    - Increasing overhead without increasing revenue
    - Growing based on ambition, not data

Small businesses fail from reckless expansion more than from competition.

The rule:

Do not expand until the core business can run without you.

III. The Power of Controlled Reinvention

Markets shift.

Economic conditions change.

Competitor strategies evolve.

A strong business reinvents deliberately, never reactively.

Reinvention may be needed when:

- Customer behavior changes
- Your industry gets disrupted
- Technology evolves
- Your business outgrows its first identity
- You want higher-value clients
- You want to pivot into a new position in the market

Reinvention is not abandoning your business.

It is upgrading it.

A smart reinvention:

- Retains the purpose
- Upgrades the systems
- Adjusts the message
- Modernizes the brand
- Keeps customer relationships intact
- Adds clarity, not confusion

IV. Relationships: The Hidden Allies of Expansion

Sun Tzu relied on alliances, intelligence, and networks.

So must a founder.

Your "business allies" include:

- Loyal customers
- Influencers or community figures
- Suppliers who trust you
- Other small business owners
- Mentors
- Skilled freelancers
- Former clients who refer new business
- Partnerships that expand your reach

A founder who builds relationships expands faster and with less effort.

A founder who isolates stays small.

V. Market Intelligence: Always Know What's Coming Next

Sun Tzu used spies.
You use information.

Market intelligence includes:

- Following industry trends
- Watching competitor behavior
- Seeing new customer patterns early
- Reading economic indicators
- Understanding where demand is rising
- Detecting when customer loyalty is weakening
- Noticing new technologies or shifts in consumer expectation

The founder who knows the real terrain wins.
The founder who guesses loses.

Every major business failure shares one thing in common:
They didn't see the change coming.

VI. Automation, Delegation & Time Freedom

Growth requires the founder to evolve out of:

- Doing everything
- Solving every problem
- Being the only expert
- Working inside the business instead of on it

Automation can handle:

- Scheduling
- Invoicing
- Basic communication
- Customer follow-ups
- Inventory updates
- Marketing sequences
- Payment processing

Delegation handles what automation cannot.

A founder's final role is:

- Direction
- Decision

- Leadership
- Strategy

If you do not delegate, you cannot scale.
If you cannot scale, you cannot expand.
If you cannot expand, you cannot win long-term.

VII. Protecting the Company as It Grows

Expansion brings risk:

- Poor hires
- Cash flow strain
- Overconfidence
- Brand dilution
- Customer experience erosion
- Loss of culture
- Loss of standards

Protect your company by:

- Reviewing numbers weekly
- Auditing systems monthly
- Listening to customers constantly
- Guarding culture fiercely
- Keeping overhead light
- Keeping quality high
- Staying paranoid about complacency

A business that grows without protection will collapse the moment pressure arrives.

VIII. The Rule of Sustainable Growth

Grow only at the speed of your systems.

Not your ego.

Not the market hype.

Not what competitors are doing.

If your systems can handle 10% more growth, grow 10%.

If they can handle 50% more, grow 50%.

Growth without infrastructure is not growth.

It is a countdown to failure.

IX. Long-Term Victory: Building Something That Outlives You

A small business becomes a lasting business when:

- It no longer depends solely on the founder
- It has systems to run itself
- It has a brand customers trust
- It has a culture employees believe in
- It has reserves, relationships, and reputation
- It has the ability to endure economic cycles
- It improves every year, even if slightly

Long-term victory comes from:

- Mastering fundamentals
- Adapting to change
- Improving every 90 days
- Keeping overhead low
- Staying humble
- Staying observant
- Staying disciplined

A business built on momentum, controlled expansion, reinvention, intelligence, and strong systems becomes unbeatable.

Conclusion

Short-term businesses chase revenue.
Long-term businesses build momentum.
Great businesses build legacy.

When you grow with discipline, expand with intelligence, protect your culture, and adapt with confidence–you create a business that lasts not just for years, but for decades.

WIN
WIN

Chapter 13

Winning Without Fighting

The greatest victory is building something that lasts.

–Coach Michael Miller

Make the Competition Irrelevant

The greatest businesses win without struggling, without begging, without chasing, and without burning themselves out.

They win because they understand something most entrepreneurs never learn:

The strongest position in business is to make your competition irrelevant.

This is the final lesson.

The highest form of victory is effortless dominance.

I. Win by Position, Not by Combat

Sun Tzu taught:
"The skillful warrior wins
before the battle is fought."

In small business terms:

You win not by out-marketing, out-pricing, or out-hustling competitors.

You win by positioning your business where no one else is standing.

You create a category of one.

You do what others are afraid to do, too lazy to do, or too blind to see.

Position beats competition.

II. Win by Reputation, Not Resistance

When your reputation becomes your shield, you no longer need to fight for business.

A reputation creates:

- Trust before the first conversation
- Word-of-mouth that beats advertising

- Loyal customers who won't leave
- Competitors who avoid competing with you directly

A small business with a powerful reputation becomes untouchable.

Your name becomes your moat.

III. Win Through Customer Devotion, Not Customer Acquisition

There is no marketing in the world more powerful than:

"I will only work with them."

Devoted customers:

- Forgive mistakes
- Promote you endlessly
- Bring you warm referrals
- Stay with you for years

Devotion is stronger than satisfaction.

Devotion is stronger than quality.

Devotion is stronger than price.

A business with customers who love it has already won.

IV. Win Through Differentiation, Not Competition

Competition is exhausting.

Differentiation is liberating.

A differentiated small business:

- Charges more
- Competes less
- Chooses its customers
- Controls its pace
- Sets its own rules

The business that is different will always beat the business that is louder.

Your goal is not to be better.

Your goal is to be unlike anyone else.

V. Win by Playing Your Game, Not Theirs

Sun Tzu warned never to fight on ground chosen by the enemy.

In business:

- Don't compete on price–unless you enjoy starving.
- Don't copy trends–unless you want to be forgotten quickly.

- Don't chase every customer–unless you like chaos.
- Don't spread yourself thin–unless you're ready to break.

Play your game:

- Your pace
- Your customers
- Your value
- Your strengths
- Your standards

Victory comes from control, not reaction.

VI. Win Through Discipline, Not Drama

Most small businesses do not die from failure.

They die from:

- Chaos
- Drama
- Indecision
- Emotional reactivity
- Poor habits
- Internal disorder

The calm, disciplined, structured business outlives the emotional one.

Discipline creates longevity.

Longevity creates dominance.

VII. Win by Outlasting Everyone

The final truth:

Most competitors don’t fail because you beat them.

They fail because they quit.

A sustainable business:

- Survives downturns
- Adapts to shifts
- Maintains cash
- Protects its systems
- Keeps its standards
- Grows slowly but surely

The business that refuses to die eventually becomes the last one standing.

This is how small businesses turn into legacy businesses.

Conclusion

The highest form of business mastery is winning without fighting.

You win by:

- Position
- Reputation

- Devotion
- Differentiation
- Discipline
- Longevity

You win by becoming the business customers trust before they ever meet you.

You win by making yourself unmatched.

You win by making yourself unavoidable.

You win by making yourself unforgettable.

This is the final lesson.

This is how to win the market without ever entering the battle.

The Entrepreneur's Charge

To build a business is to accept responsibility.

Responsibility for decisions.
Responsibility for employees.
Responsibility for customers who place their trust in your work.

Entrepreneurship is often portrayed as freedom.

In reality, it is discipline.

It demands preparation when others improvise.
Patience when others rush.
Clarity when circumstances are uncertain.

Markets will change.
Competitors will appear.
Economic cycles will rise and fall.

But businesses built on strong principles endure.

Build carefully.
Lead responsibly.
Protect your reputation.
Guard your standards.

Because the greatest measure of a business is not how quickly it grows, but how long it lasts.

Build something that endures.

Strategic Influences

The ideas presented in this book draw inspiration from a long tradition of thinking about leadership, preparation, and competitive strategy.

One of the most enduring works in this tradition is *The Art of War*, attributed to the ancient Chinese strategist Sun Tzu. Written more than two thousand years ago, it examined how leaders prepare for conflict, understand their opponents, and position themselves for success before competition begins.

Although originally written in a military context, its principles have influenced leaders in fields as diverse as politics, business, athletics, and organizational leadership.

This book applies those strategic ideas to the modern challenge of building and sustaining a small business. While the arena has changed, the underlying principles of preparation, discipline, awareness, and leadership remain remarkably consistent across centuries.

Epilogue

The world of business will continue to change.

Technologies will evolve. Markets will shift. New competitors will emerge.

But the core principles that sustain strong businesses remain remarkably constant.

Preparation still matters. Leadership still matters. Reputation still matters. Discipline still matters.

Entrepreneurs who focus only on growth often build fragile organizations. Entrepreneurs who focus on building strong systems, clear leadership, and disciplined cultures create businesses capable of enduring uncertainty.

A successful business is not measured solely by revenue. It is measured by resilience, by the trust it earns from customers, and by the stability it creates for the people who depend on it.

Markets reward those who prepare carefully, act thoughtfully, and persist when conditions become difficult.

Those who build with patience and clarity often discover that the greatest advantage in business is not speed, but endurance.

About the Author

Dr. Michael Miller is an author, businessman, educator, and strategist whose work focuses on leadership, discipline, negotiation, and long-term success. Over the course of his career, he has owned and operated businesses, managed construction and real estate projects, worked in higher education administration, and mentored entrepreneurs and professionals from a wide range of industries.

Dr. Miller is the author of more than twenty books exploring strategy, business, leadership, psychology, and personal development. His writing is known for its direct, practical style–combining real-world experience with a strong emphasis on discipline, positioning, and results.

In addition to his work as an author and speaker, Dr. Miller owns and operates a successful barbershop business in Los Angeles, California. His recently published book, *The Art of the Chair*, has been well received within the barbering industry and has been featured as an award and prize item at major barber battle competitions and industry events. He has also served as a keynote speaker for large barbering events, addressing students and professionals on leadership, branding, discipline, and long-term success in business.

Beyond his professional work, Dr. Miller remains involved in community and nonprofit efforts, including volunteer outreach work in Watts, Compton, and South Los Angeles. He is also the founder of a nonprofit dog rescue organization, reflecting his belief that leadership and success should ultimately create opportunity, stability, and compassion for others.